We loved you Before

Written By: Leah R. Caldwell
Illustrated by: Belina Wright
Cover Art by: Edison Liburd

One Connect LRC Publishing

Copyright © 2025 by Leah R. Caldwell

All rights reserved. No part of this book may be reproduced or used in any manner without written permission of the copyright owner, except for the use of brief quotations in a book review, commentary, or educational setting.

This is a work of fiction. Any resemblance to actual persons, living or dead, or real events is purely coincidental.

Scripture: Psalm 139:13-14 (King James Version)

Author: Leah R. Caldwell
Email: leahrcaldwell50@gmail.com

Cover Art by: Edison Liburd

Book Formatting, Illustrations, and Layout by:
Belina Wright
Email: belina@bwrightart.com

First paperback edition 2025
Published by One Connect LRC Publishing

ISBN: 979-8-9856576-1-6 (Paperback)

For permissions or inquiries, please contact:
leahrcaldwell@icloud.com

In loving memory of my mother, Ann M. Phelps, a gifted writer of Christian stories and poems. I am blessed to have had a mom who cherished the written and spoken word, inspiring me to do the same. This book is a tribute to her love, faith, and storytelling.
-Leah

Thank you God for this gift. Thank you Stephen, Aaron, Avani, Alex and Adrianna for your love and support.
-Belina

God knew you long before,
You were even but a seed.
Before you were a thought,
I knew you well indeed.

We loved you long before
The womb of your conception.

Our plans were all laid out
Before your grand reception.

We protected you before—
Dangers seen and those unseen,
When you were just an embryo,
When you were just a gene.

We comforted you before
Any pain you may have felt.
Our loving arms embraced you
When in the womb you dwelt.

We prayed for you before
Your eyes were ever opened,
Your ears had ever heard,
Your lips had ever spoken.

We forgave you long before
Your head came down its path.
We washed you in our love
Before your very first bath.

We cried for you before
You laid upon mom's breast.
Before you called her Mom,
We knew that we were blessed.

We prepared for you before —
A place for you to grow.
A home that we will share,
Where love will always flow.

"For thou hast possessed my reins: Thou hast covered me in my mother's womb. I will praise thee; for I am fearfully and wonderfully made: Marvellous are thy works; And that my soul knoweth right well."
Psalm 139:13-14 KJV

About the Author

Leah R. Caldwell is a devoted mother, grandmother, and mentor who finds joy in inspiring young minds. She loves jazz, cycling, reading, and spending time by the water.

About the Illustrator

Belina Buisson-Wright is a native Floridian of Haitian American descent. Wright is a self-taught artist that believes her ability to paint is a God-given gift. Her art is strongly influenced by her Haitian and African-American heritage. She tries to capture its vibrancy in her work. She enjoys painting people in their element - from the extreme to the simple and mundane. She resides in Central Florida with her husband, Stephen, and their four children.

Draw a picture of your family!

www.ingramcontent.com/pod-product-compliance
Lightning Source LLC
Chambersburg PA
CBHW042133070426
42453CB00002BA/78